Food

CORN

Margaret Hall

Heinemann Library
Chicago, Illinois

Printed in Hong Kong
Map illustration by Kimberly Saar/Heinemann Library

06 05 04 03 02
10 9 8 7 6 5 4 3 2 1

Library of Congress Cataloging-in-Publication Data
Hall, Margaret, 1947-
  Corn / Margaret Hall.
     v. cm. -- (Food)
Includes bibliographical references and index.
Contents: What is corn? -- Kinds of corn -- In the past -- Around the
world -- Looking at corn -- Planting corn -- How corn grows --
Harvesting corn -- Corn at the factory -- Corn on the table -- Good for
you -- Healthy eating -- Corn recipe.
  ISBN 1-58810-617-9
  1. Cookery (Corn)--Juvenile literature. 2. Corn--Juvenile literature.
[1. Corn.] I. Title. II. Series.
  TX809.M2 H35 2002
  641.6'315--dc21

2002000468

Acknowledgments
The author and publisher are grateful to the following for permission to reproduce copyright material:

Cover photograph by Richard T. Nowitz/Corbis

pp. 4, 25 Michael Newman/Photo Edit, Inc.; p. 4tl Kimberly Saar/Heinemann Library; p. 5 Larry Luxner;
pp. 6, 18, 19 Lynn M. Stone; p. 7 John Mantel/Bruce Coleman, Inc.; p. 8 Bettman/Corbis; p. 9 The Granger
Collection, New York; p. 10 Jose Carillo/Photo Edit, Inc.; p. 12 Tony Freeman/Photo Edit, Inc.; p. 13 David
Young-Wolff/Photo Edit, Inc.; p. 14 Debra Ferguson/AgStockUSA; p. 15 Liba Taylor/Corbis; pp. 16, 17 Inga
Spence/Visuals Unlimited; p. 20 David Frazier Photo Library; p. 21 Jack Ballard/Visuals Unlimited; Felica
Martinez/Photo Edit, Inc.; p. 23 Danielle B. Hayes/Omni-Photo Communications; p. 24 Myrleen Ferguson
Cate/Photo Edit, Inc.; pp. 28, 29 Eric Anderson/Visuals Unlimited

Every effort has been made to contact copyright holders of any material reproduced in this book.
Any omissions will be rectified in subsequent printings if notice is given to the publisher.

Some words are shown in bold, **like this.** You can
find out what they mean by looking in the glossary.

Contents

What Is Corn?

Corn is a tall, leafy plant that belongs to the grass family. A full-grown corn plant is taller than an adult person! People eat the seeds of the corn plant.

Some people grow corn in their gardens. They eat this corn themselves. But farmers grow most of the world's corn in huge fields as a **crop** to sell.

Kinds of Corn

There are many different kinds of corn. The corn we eat is **sweet corn. Dent corn** is used to feed **livestock.** It gets its name from the dent in each **kernel.**

Popcorn is a special kind of corn that **explodes** when it is heated. Flint corn is also called **Indian corn.** It has red, blue, and purple kernels!

In the Past

Corn grew **wild** in Mexico thousands of years ago. People ate this wild corn. Then they started planting the seeds to grow corn as a **crop.**

Native Americans had a special way to plant corn. They put dead fish and corn seeds into small mounds of dirt. The **nutrients** in the fish helped the corn grow better.

Around the World

Long ago, corn only grew in North and South America. Today it is grown all around the world. In some places, corn is still called by its Native American name: maize.

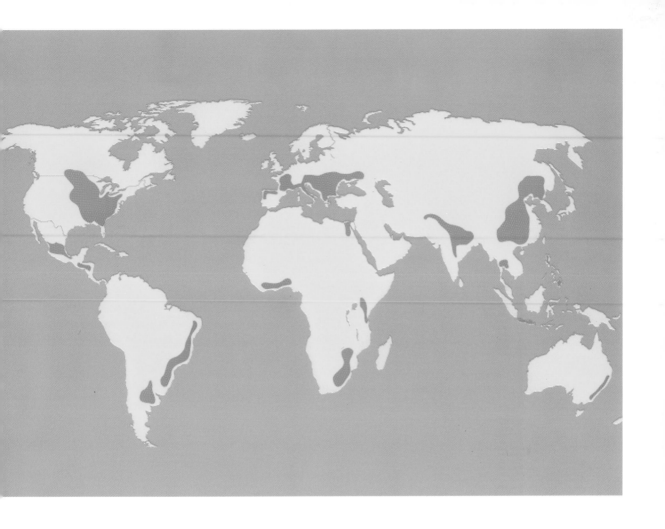

On this map, the places where the most corn is grown are shown in red. Corn grows best in places that have warm summers with lots of rain.

Looking at Corn

A corn plant has a tall, leafy stem called a **stalk. Corncobs** grow along the stalk. Each corncob is protected by a **husk.**

leaf

stalk

Inside the husk, **kernels** grow in rows on the corncob. People eat just the kernels. Some animals eat the kernels and the corncob, too.

kernel

husk

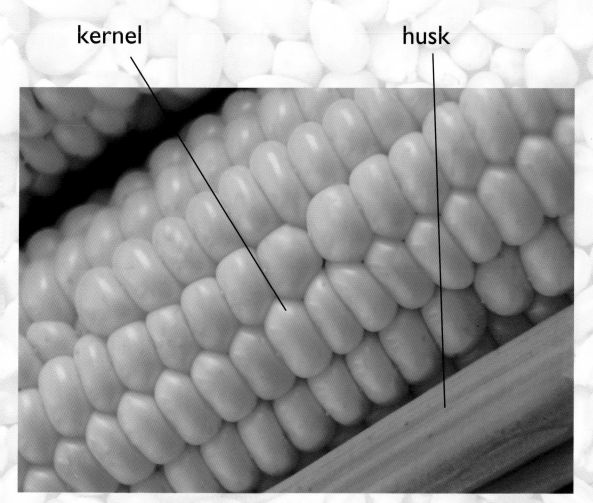

13

Planting Corn

Each **kernel** of corn is a seed that can grow into a new corn plant. Farmers use machines to plant the seeds in long, straight rows.

Like all plants, corn needs sunshine,
nutrients, and water. Some kinds of corn
are fully grown in about 60 days. Other
kinds need to grow for many months.

How Corn Grows

Each corn **stalk** has a **tassel** at the top. Tiny flowers grow on the tassel. The wind carries **pollen** from the flowers to the **corn silk** at the end of each **corncob.**

When the pollen travels down the **strands** of corn silk, **kernels** start to grow. One corncob can have more than 1,000 kernels!

Harvesting Corn

The corn is ready to **harvest** when the **corn silk** turns brown. Most farmers use machines to pick the corn. Some machines even cut the **kernels** off the **corncobs.**

Farmers **store** some corn to use for feeding **livestock**. They sell the rest of the corn to factories to be **processed.**

Processing Corn

Some corn **kernels** are **canned** or frozen. Other corn is dried and ground to make **cornmeal.** Corn and other **ingredients** can be cooked together, then shaped and toasted to make cereal.

Corn kernels are separated into parts, too. The **corn oil** is squeezed out. Cornstarch and corn syrup are other parts that are **processed** to use in foods.

Corn on the Table

People eat corn by itself as popcorn, corn on the cob, **canned** corn, and frozen corn. They also eat cereal, muffins, and bread made from corn or **cornmeal.**

Margarine and salad dressings often contain **corn oil.** Cornstarch and corn syrup are used in cookies and other desserts. Corn is even an **ingredient** in candy and gum!

Good for You

Foods like corn are called **carbohydrates.** Carbohydrates help your body produce **energy.** You need this energy to be able to move and grow.

Corn also has small amounts of other important **nutrients** and **vitamins.** They help your body stay strong and healthy.

Healthy Eating

The food guide **pyramid** shows how much of each different kind of food you should eat every day.

All of the food groups are important, but your body needs more of some foods than others.

You should eat more of the foods at the bottom and middle of the pyramid. You should eat less of the foods at the top.

Corn by itself is in the vegetable group. Your body needs three servings of vegetables each day. Many foods made from corn are in the **grain** group. Your body needs six servings of grains each day.

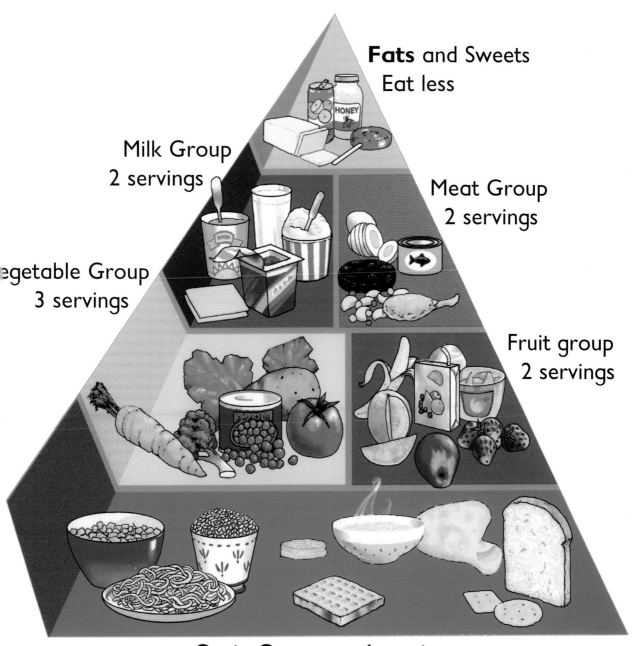

Fats and Sweets
Eat less

Milk Group
2 servings

Meat Group
2 servings

Vegetable Group
3 servings

Fruit group
2 servings

Grain Group   6 servings

Based on the Food Guide Pyramid for Young Children, U.S. Department of Agriculture, Center for Nutrition Policy and Promotion, March 1999.

Double Corn Cornbread Recipe

You will need:

1 cup (140 g) **cornmeal**

½ cup (65 g) flour

1 tablespoon baking powder

2 tablespoons sugar

½ teaspoon salt

½ teaspoon baking soda

Ask an adult to help you!

½ cup (120 ml) **corn oil**

1 cup milk

2 eggs

11-ounce (320-g) can whole-**kernel** corn, drained

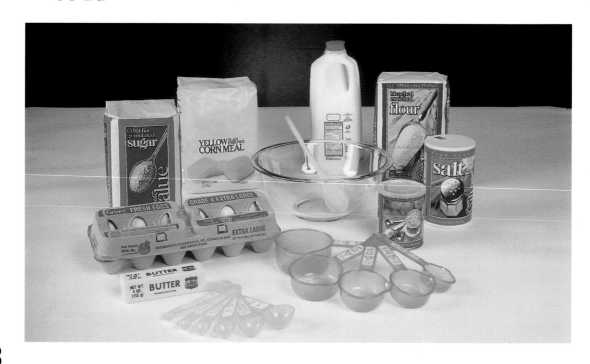

1. Mix the cornmeal, flour, baking powder, sugar, salt, and baking soda together in a bowl.
2. In another bowl, mix the oil, milk, and eggs.

3. Pour the wet **ingredients** into the dry ingredients and stir until evenly mixed.
4. Add the corn kernels and stir again.
5. Pour into a greased 9-inch square pan. Bake at 425°F (220°C) for 25 minutes.

Glossary

can to save for eating later by putting in a can

carbohydrate part of some foods that the body uses to make energy

corncob part of the corn plant on which kernels grow

cornmeal dried, ground corn used to make bread and muffins

corn oil oil squeezed from kernels of corn

corn silk long, soft strands that grow at the top of a corncob

crop plants raised to eat or to sell to others

dent corn corn used to feed livestock

energy power to do things

explode to blow up

fat part of some foods that the body uses to make energy and keep warm

grain seed of a cereal plant

harvest to gather or bring in crops

husk leaves that cover a corncob

Indian corn corn with red, blue, and purple kernels; also called flint corn

ingredient part of a mixture

kernel corn seed; the part of the corn plant that is eaten by people

livestock farm animals such as cattle and pigs

nutrient food that plants or people need to grow and be healthy

pollen tiny yellow specks on a flower that help make seeds

process to cook or treat in a certain way to make a new kind of food or drink

pyramid shape with a flat bottom and three sides with edges that come to a point

ripe completely grown

stalk thick stem that holds leaves and fruit of a plant

store to save to use later

strand long, thin tube

sweet corn kind of corn eaten by people

tassel flower and stem that grow at the top of a corn plant

vitamin something the body needs to grow and stay healthy

wild not planted by people

More Books to Read

Burckhardt, Ann L. *Corn.* Mankato, Minn.: Bridgestone Books, 1996.

Pickering, Robin. *I Like Corn.* Danbury, Conn.: Children's Press, 2000.

Royston, Angela. *Eat Well.* Chicago: Heinemann Library, 2000.

Index